JUNIOR PET CARE

GUINEA PIGS

ZUZA VRBOVA

Photography Susan C. Miller
Illustration Robert McAulay, Hugh Nicholas
Reading and Child Psychology Consultant
Dr. David Lewis

ACKNOWLEDGMENTS

With special thanks to Jenny Toft, Pet Bowl;
Pat and Tony Lear;
Keith Berry;
and especially to Hector and Horace and Marilyn and
Alex Hunt.

Library of Congress #89-52055

Distributed in the UNITED STATES by T.F.H. Publications, Inc., One T.F.H. Plaza, Neptune City, NJ 07753; in CANADA to the Pet Trade by H & L Pet Supplies Inc., 27 Kingston Crescent, Kitchener, Ontario N2B 2T6; Rolf C. Hagen Ltd., 3225 Sartelon Street, Montreal 382 Quebec; in CANADA to the Book Trade by Macmillan of Canada (A Division of Canada Publishing Corporation), 164 Commander Boulevard, Agincourt, Ontario M1S 3C7; in ENGLAND by T.F.H. Publications, The Spinney, Parklands, Portsmouth PO7 6AR; in AUSTRALIA AND THE SOUTH PACIFIC by T.F.H. (Australia) Pty. Ltd., Box 149, Brookvale 2100 N.S.W., Australia; in NEW ZEALAND by Ross Haines & Son, Ltd., 82 D Elizabeth Knox Place, Panmure, Auckland, New Zealand; in the PHILIPPINES by Bio-Research, 5 Lippay Street, San Lorenzo Village, Makati Rizal; in SOUTH AFRICA by Multipet Pty. Ltd., Box 235 New Germany, South Africa 3620. Published by T.F.H. Publications, Inc. Manufactured in the United States of America by T.F.H. Publications, Inc.

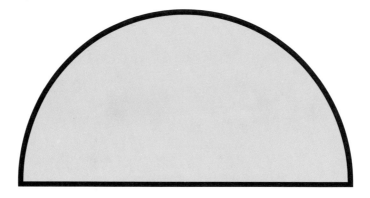

CONTENTS

NOTE TO PARENTS

Guinea pigs are a perfect first pet for a child. As guinea pigs are affectionate and enjoy being handled, children can start learning how to look after guinea pigs themselves from a young age. *Guinea Pigs* has been specially written and designed for children of 7 years of age and older. This book will help them learn how to hold and feed a guinea pig and be in charge of its daily care.

THE NATURE OF
A GUINEA PIG

Guinea pigs are furry, friendly animals. They like being cuddled and petted. They even enjoy being carried around, although you must be careful not to squeeze your guinea pig too tightly.

Guinea pigs are not pigs. The name 'pig' might have arisen because guinea pigs sometimes make soft squeaking, squealing or grunting noises that sound rather like a pig, but they are not as loud as a pig's grunt. Also, a guinea pig's chubby body and style of walking is a little pig-like. Another name for a guinea pig is **cavy.**

Guinea pigs have a calm manner. They like people and once they have settled into a new home, they soon become very tame.

Guinea pigs can live for about six years. They are very easy to look after.

Guinea pigs in the wild

Guinea pigs come from South America. Long before the discovery of America, South American Indians called the Incas kept guinea pigs in their homes. Explorers brought guinea pigs home as pets for their children. At first they were very expensive and only rich people could afford them. Wild guinea pigs still live in the grasslands of South America. They stay close together in groups. They search for food and they make paths in the tall grass, rather like a maze. They can run away fast and they warn each other if there is any danger by whistling or squeaking. If they are chased by a bigger animal they usually hide or else they lie completely still and hope they will not be seen.

CHOOSING
A GUINEA PIG

The ideal place to buy a guinea pig is a pet store. When a guinea pig is about six to eight weeks old, it will be ready to go to its new home. At this age it will be able to live on its own and will settle well in a new home. It will soon become very tame.

Young guinea pigs are especially cute. Unlike human babies, guinea pigs are born with a full set of teeth. They can walk around almost as soon as they are born and they can eat solid food when they are only a few days old.

Guinea pigs are such friendly animals that one guinea pig kept on its own may become very lonely. It will need a good deal of attention from you to keep it happy.

It is often better to buy two guinea pigs so that they can keep each other company. If you do decide to buy two guinea pigs, either buy two female guinea pigs or two male guinea pigs. Female guinea pigs are less likely to fight with each other when they grow up.

A male guinea pig is called a **boar** and a female guinea pig is called a **sow.** They both make good pets, although males may be slightly less shy.

Kinds of guinea pigs

Guinea pigs come in several different coat types and in lots of different colors and markings. Before you buy your guinea pig you will have to decide which kind you would like.

The coat can be smooth and short-

A Chocolate-colored guinea pig with a smooth short-haired coat (above).

14

A rosetted rough-coated tortoise shell and white guinea pig (left).

A short-haired guinea pig with a smooth deep black coat (right).

A smooth, short-haired guinea pig that is cream colored all over, with dark eyes (left).

haired, rough-haired, with the fur sticking up in fluffy rosettes all over the body, or else simply long-haired.

When you choose your guinea pig, remember that the ones with a smooth or a rosetted coat are the easiest to keep clean and well groomed. The fur of long-haired guinea pigs needs brushing and cleaning every day.

A long-haired guinea pig is not a beginner's guinea pig. It always needs lots of daily care and attention because the hair of a long-haired guinea pig needs to be brushed and styled every day—just as our hair needs to be combed frequently. So, unless you have plenty of time to groom your new guinea pig, it is best not to buy a long-haired one at first.

Selecting a good guinea pig

At the pet store, look at the guinea pigs carefully and watch them for a few minutes. Reach out towards a youngster that you particularly like. If it is interested in your hand but seems to be a bit shy, it will probably grow into a very tame and friendly guinea pig.

Ask the store assistant to pick up the guinea pig before you decide to buy it. You can then examine it more

closely. It should be alert, with bright, clear eyes. Its body should feel sturdy and firm. The nails should not be overgrown. The coat should be thick and glossy, with no bald patches. Check that the guinea pig has clean ears and a dry nose.

When you look at the guinea pig you will quickly notice that guinea pigs do not have tails. They have four toes on the front feet and only three toes on the back feet.

Bringing your guinea pig home

When you go to buy your new pet remember to bring a box with you to carry the guinea pig home in. The size of the box is important. It must not be too small, but a great big box would allow the guinea pig to run around in fright and it might hurt itself. The guinea pig should fit snugly in the box and the box should have holes in the sides or top so your pet can breathe.

A guinea pig's teeth

The guinea pig in this picture has overgrown teeth.

Our teeth stop growing as soon as they have reached the right size. Guinea pigs have to file their teeth down all the time by chewing on hard objects, like a piece of wood. Pet guinea pigs need a gnawing block to keep their front teeth trim. Your pet store should have a suitable chew available. Their grinding teeth for chewing up their food are at the back of their cheeks.

Once or twice a year you should check your guinea pig's teeth. It's a bit like you going to the dentist for a check-up. With a guinea pig you must make sure that the teeth have not grown too long. If they are overgrown, it might stop your guinea pig from being able to eat. If you think that your guinea pig's teeth might be too long, ask a grown-up to help you take it to a veterinarian to have its teeth clipped.

A HOME FOR YOUR GUINEA PIG

Pet guinea pigs live in sturdy hutches or cages. A wooden hutch is the best kind of home for a guinea pig because it has more space than a cage.

A hutch often has two rooms—a living room and a bedroom for the guinea pigs.

Guinea pigs like to have a quiet place to relax in (below).

The living area of the hutch usually has a wire mesh front, making a light and airy place for the guinea pigs during the day. The food bowl is kept in the living room and the water bottle can be attached to the wire mesh.

The bedroom part of the hutch usually has a solid wooden front, making it a restful retreat during the day and a cozy den where the guinea pigs can go to sleep at night.

Water must always be within a guinea pig's reach. It is best to provide water in a drip bottle (left).

There is a hole that forms an archway between the two rooms of the hutch so that guinea pigs can easily move from one room to another whenever they like.

There
are several dif-
ferent kinds of hutches that
you can buy. When you choose one,
make sure it is big enough for your
guinea pigs to live in comfortably.

The hutches that have a front door
to each of the two compartments are
easier to clean. Ideally, the roof of the
hutch should be sloping and over-
hang the front to protect the guinea
pigs in bad weather. Roofs of our
houses are often sloped for the same
reason.

Where
to keep the hutch
If you live in a warm place you can keep the hutch outside all year round. But, if you are in an area that is cold in winter, you should put the hutch in a shed or a utility room then, because guinea pigs do not like very cold weather.

If you let your guinea pig freely explore the garden for a while, watch it carefully to make sure it does not escape or get lost and protect it from any cats and dogs. It will probably try to scurry toward a low hedge or wall. It will push through tall grass and make runways as it would do in the wild. The blades of grass will naturally groom the guinea pig, making its coat sleek and shiny.

Your guinea pig's bed

A guinea pig needs material in the hutch to keep warm and dry and to make a bed out of.

Wood shavings make an ideal flooring material in a hutch. They can be spread around the hutch luxuriously to make a comfortable, fitted carpet for the guinea pig's feet.

Put three or four handfuls of sweet-smelling fresh hay on top of the wood shavings in the bedroom part of the hutch. Your guinea pig will be able to snuggle down in this at night and will nibble at the tips of the hay.

A grazing ark

If you keep your guinea pigs in a hutch without an enclosure, they will need to spend some time in a grazing ark. This is sometimes also called a **run.** It is a wooden-framed cage covered with wire mesh.

Guinea pigs like spending the day in a run. They can enjoy the fresh air in the spring and summer and they can

eat the grass growing on the floor of the run. You can move the run from place to place on the lawn so that they have fresh grass every day.

Guinea pigs do not make underground tunnels as rabbits do, so they cannot escape from the run.

Like the hutch, a part of the run should be covered, and the floor should be lined with fresh hay. The guinea pigs can use this area to retreat into if they are frightened or need a rest. They can also use it as a shelter if it starts to rain or for shade if it is too hot and sunny.

Indoor exercise

Sometimes it is too cold and wet to let your guinea pigs graze outside. But guinea pigs like to trot around and should not be shut in a hutch for long.

You can either let your guinea pigs wander through the house for a little while, keeping an eye on them all the time, or you can put them in an indoor play pen. This is a bit like a baby's play pen. It is a safe area for the guinea pigs to play in, indoors.

The wooden frame of the run should be sturdy enough to rest securely on the ground (left) so that your guinea pigs cannot crawl out underneath.

An outdoor enclosure

If you have enough space in your backyard you can fence off part of the lawn around the hutch so that your guinea pigs can go in and out whenever they please.

You can fix a ramp from the hutch to the ground to make it easy for your guinea pigs to leave the hutch. Then they can spend the day roaming around in their own little patch. They will feel safe there and can have lots of fun.

It is a good idea to put a wooden log in the enclosure for the guinea pigs to gnaw on. You can make the enclosure into an exciting part of the garden for you, too. Throw in some wildflower seeds that will grow and look very beautiful and at the same time provide some of your guinea pigs' favorite food. Another idea is to make a rock garden in the enclosure for the guinea pigs to scamper about on and perhaps find interesting garden plants to eat.

FEEDING
YOUR GUINEA PIG

In their natural homelands wild guinea pigs eat the leaves, stems and seeds of different kinds of grasses. If they can find them, guinea pigs also like plants such as cow parsley, dock, shepherd's purse, plantain and perhaps local treats like corn on the cob.

Pet guinea pigs eat grass, hay, cereal and plenty of fresh vegetables. Guinea pigs are creatures of habit. They like to be fed at a regular time twice a day. They are like us in a way. They have breakfast and an evening meal.

Because guinea pigs have good ears, you will soon notice that your pet will listen for your footsteps at meal times. It will probably come out to greet you, making little grunting sounds, especially if it is hungry.

Guinea pigs dislike big changes in their lives, so when you first buy your guinea pig, ask the pet store keeper what kinds of food it has been eating.

At first, you can give it similar kinds of food until it has settled into its new home. Then, after a while you can start to explore your guinea pig's taste and you will soon find out what its favorite foods are.

Cereal is an important part of a guinea pig's food. It is best to give cereal in the morning—just like you might have cereal for breakfast. Guinea pig cereal is slightly different from ours. You can buy a specially-prepared mix of cereal food for guinea pigs from pet stores. It is made of a variety of grains, wholemeal bread and bran. It has the same food value as the grass seeds that a guinea pig would eat in the wild.

Making a mash

You can either give the cereal food to your guinea pig as it comes—dry—or make a crumbly mash with it by mixing it with hot or cold milk or water. Remember to wash the bowls after

feeding time—just like we have to wash the dishes after a meal.

Guinea pigs and vitamin C

To stay healthy guinea pigs need food which contains goodness in the form of vitamin C. We need this vitamin to stay healthy too. We cannot see vitamin C, but we know it is present in lots of different kinds of food which your guinea pig will like. All kinds of fruits and vegetables contain vitamin C. Carrots, cauliflower, cabbage and broccoli are just a few of the many options.

Putting a few vitamin drops into the water bottle (above) ensures your guinea pig stays fit and healthy. You can buy vitamin drops from your local pet store.

Broccoli is especially high in vitamins, and outside leaves of a cauliflower are good too. We usually throw cauliflower leaves away but your guinea pig will love to eat them. Guinea pigs like apples and other pieces of fruit and welcome a change from day to day. Carrots, besides being good for your guinea pig to eat, are a hard food that will help to keep its teeth from growing too long.

Eating their food

Guinea pigs do not use their front feet as hands, so they find food easier to eat if it is cut into small chunks. When a guinea pig eats, it simply squats before the food and nibbles. Sometimes a guinea pig will carry a special treat, such as a favorite leaf, away from the feeding dish and find a quiet corner to eat it in peace. Food is always carried in the guinea pig's mouth.

Fresh hay is another important part of a guinea pig's needs. You can

Apples, carrots, celery, cauliflower and cauliflower leaves (below) are all good for your guinea pig.

Picking flowers
for your guinea
pig is fun.
Nasturtiums
and sweet peas
(below) are just
two kinds of
flowers that
guinea pigs like
to eat.

buy fresh hay from your local pet store. Guinea pigs are like horses. They will nibble on some grass or hay throughout the day and even at night. Hay is important for a guinea pig in several ways. Nibbling hay stops a guinea pig from becoming bored. A guinea pig often eats the fresh tips of the hay and then makes the stalks into a cozy warm bed like eiderdown, an ideal bedding material.

It is best to use heavy feeding pots that you can buy from a pet store to put your guinea pig's food in. This will prevent the food bowls being tipped over.

HANDLING AND
GENERAL CARE

When you bring your new guinea pig home, it may be nervous at first. It may not be used to being handled. Also, the journey and the new surroundings may be frightening for a young guinea pig.

If you stroke it, talk to it and gently try to play with it every day it will soon settle in. It will quickly become tame and learn to recognize your voice, coming to greet you as you approach the hutch.

In turn, you will start to understand your guinea pig's ways and get to know what the little sounds it makes mean. Some grunts might mean that the guinea pig is happy about the food it is eating, and other sounds might mean it is hungry or frightened.

Picking up a guinea pig

A grown-up should show you how to hold a guinea pig correctly. The best way is to slide one hand under its body and use the other hand to steady the guinea pig. Then lift it up gently, making sure it is secure in your arms.

You should always handle your guinea pig gently and make sure your friends do the same. If you are gentle with your guinea pig, it will soon become tame and friendly. Never pick a guinea pig up by the scruff of the neck or grab it tightly round the middle.

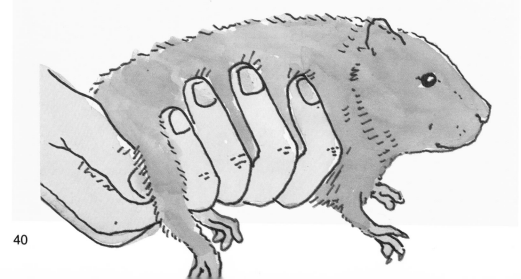

It is best to use both your hands when you first learn how to pick up your guinea pig.

The safest way to learn how to handle your guinea pig well is while you are sitting on the ground. This way there is no chance of your dropping it.

Grooming

You can brush your guinea pig's coat with a soft baby's brush or a tooth-brush. Short-haired guinea pigs do not need to be groomed, but if your guinea pig is a long-coated one, grooming is an important part of its daily care. Guinea pigs with fluffy, rosetted coats need regular grooming too.

Trimming the claws

When your guinea pig is about one year old, it might need to have its nails trimmed. A grown-up or a veterinarian should do this, because it can be difficult. Trimming the claws does not hurt a guinea pig if it is done properly. But if the nails are trimmed too short they might bleed; this will be painful for the guinea pig.

Going on vacation

If you go away for more than two days you must make sure your guinea pig is looked after by someone who knows how to take care of it. You may be able to board your pet at the shop of the pet dealer from whom you bought your guinea pig.

Cleaning out the hutch

Your guinea pig's hutch needs to be cleaned out thoroughly at least once a week. Besides simply changing the bedding material, the hutch will also need to be scrubbed thoroughly three or four times a year. Try to do this on a sunny day so that you can let the hutch dry out completely in the sun. Putting your guinea pig back into a damp hutch could cause it to catch a cold.

COMMON GUINEA PIG AILMENTS

If you look after your guinea pig well, feed it properly and make sure it is comfortable, it will probably stay healthy. But, like us all, even a well cared for guinea pig may have an occasional illness or have an accident. Guinea pigs that are seriously ill seem very quickly to lose the will to live.

If you think your guinea pig might be suffering from an illness, the best thing to do is to ask a grown-up to help you take it to a veterinarian. The most important thing to know about treating an ill guinea pig is that guinea pigs are allergic to a drug called **penicillin.** If they are given this medication, they will die. You should always seek proper advice rather than trying to treat your pet yourself.

Teeth

If a guinea pig accidentally falls, it might break its front teeth. They will easily grow again, but until they do, they should be trimmed by a veterinarian so that both the front teeth are the same size.

Eye injuries

A stalk of hay might poke a young guinea pig in the eye. The eye usually recovers on its own, but if the eye looks damaged—it may be a milky color—make sure that the stalk is not still in the guinea pig's eye. Take the guinea pig to the veterinarian, who will probably give it some eye ointment.

Skin troubles

If your guinea pig looks as though it is scratching itself more than usual and starts to lose small patches of hair, it might have **mites**. These are tiny animals that burrow under the surface of the skin. Mites are similar to lice and are sometimes found in hay. Take your guinea pig to a veterinarian, who will probably give you a special soap to wash the guinea pig with.

Vitamin C deficiency

Guinea pigs that do not have enough vitamin C in their food can well get an unhealthy skin condition. This is called **scurvy**. They are also more likely to catch colds. Such guinea pigs might not be eating properly because of overgrown teeth.

Stripping hair

Some guinea pigs start to pick at their hair if they are bored. The problem may be caused if the guinea pig does not have enough hay to chew. A guinea pig with this habit might well be lonely and should be kept with another guinea pig, rather than on its own, and played with as much as possible. An interesting hutch or enclosure for the guinea pig to explore helps, too.

Pneumonia

If your guinea pig sits hunched up in a corner of the hutch, looking unhappy, and has fast, noisy breathing, it probably has a bad cold or even pneumonia. The best treatment you can give is warmth and lots of water with a vitamin supplement and sugar in it. Your veterinarian will provide medicine for your pet for this serious illness.

GLOSSARY

Boar A male guinea pig.

Cavy Another name for a guinea pig.

Rosette Similar to a cowlick in human hair, a rosette looks like a circle, as all the hair is pushed out from the center in a flower-like spiral shape.

Run A wooden-framed cage with no bottom, used to allow the guinea pig to graze on fresh grass.

Scurvy A skin disease caused by a lack of vitamin C in the guinea pig's diet.

Sow A female guinea pig.